The next step await
I'm obedient. So, I give you this gift in
its purest form. Authentic and unfiltered.
As it was given to me.

--Selwyn Collins

S E L W Y N   A.   C O L L I N S

THE
EartHeart Knows
WHO YOU ARE

It can feel your presence and your energy. It's like you're a part of it, and it's a part of you. You're connected to the earth through your heart, and it's connected to you.

**Written & Illustrated
by Selwyn A. Collins**

I Am

I am that I am you.
But you are not me.
I am the universe.
But the universe is not me.
I am the beginning.
But the beginning is not me.

I am that I am your consciousness.
But your consciousness is not me.
I am all able.
But all that is able is not me.
I am the end.
But the end is not me.

It is I who found you,
and awaits you to find me.

Marjorie Angela Collins

She who gave birth to me, spoke to me in a tone only a child who is intimate with love could truly understand.

My dearest mother, I am eternally grateful for your love, your compassion, and your will. I hear the sound of your voice, and I'm thrilled. I am still. You calm me, then hope and peace are with me.

Often, I wonder what you knew then that you took the care and time to implant certain seeds in me. What do you know about preparation, patience, and harvests?

I understand a mother's love, but where did you find the grace and the strength to listen to so many questions, many very strange coming from a child? How could you love so completely and purely that even your admonitions and whippings were understood?

Now I understand why I arrived and found everyone calling you 'M'. It wasn't for Marjorie, though I thought it meant mother. Now I am convinced it's for Magnificent.

I love you M. I love you eternally.

Edwin Albert Collins
1919 - 1993

To my father

EDWIN ALBERT COLLINS
Your gracious life inspired in me a thirst to understand
the dramatic and intimate dance
between synchronicity and mortality.

Your transition filled me with much grief, but it also
introduced me to a realm within and unlocked a
passion for getting to know myself.

The eartHeart Knows Who You Are
© Copyright 2022 by Selwyn A. Collins.

ISBN: 978-0-9851150-4-3

Cover design: Sade Barrow-Brown.
Author's photo credit: Byron Henry.
Other photo credit: Joy Bobb-Semple.

ACKNOWLEDGEMENTS

I would like to first thank my mother for always being there for me with her unconditional love and support. I could not have completed this book without her encouragement through those very challenging times.

I cannot find the words to express my gratitude to Gillian Thomas for her love and unwavering support. By urging me to reprint 'The eartHeart Knows,' it got me thinking and motivated me to write this new book, 'The eartHeart Knows Who You Are.'

Many thanks to Carl Agard, Dr. Sandie Anderson, Holly Harper, Mosa Telford, and Patrick Nicholson for encouraging me to write this new book. It's been a labor of love, and I hope you enjoy reading it as much as I enjoyed writing it.

From Their Hearts

"The "eartHeart Knows" is a mirror to our own hearts.
"It takes us on a journey of introspection, yet it is hopeful, uplifting and inspiring..."

-- Carl Agard

"A lovely book of poetry, paired with beautiful imagery. Perfect for an afternoon read with a loved one and some tea."

-- Dr. Sandile Hlatshwayo, Economist, IMF

"The eartHeart Knows is not your average book of affirmations. It's like having a deck of oracle cards in hand. Open it up to a random page, and the one meditation that pulls you in tells you exactly where you are in your life and, if you're truly tapped in.
Exactly what you need to know to make progress."

-- Gillian Thomas

"The eartHeart Knows, what do we know? If after reading this book we do not ponder on this, then... Read it and go deep in yourself. A book to take you on a journey to a good place. Take a read."

-- Kay Gray

The eartHeart Knows Who You Are

"The eartHeart Knows is a reminder of how much power a well-crafted arrangement of words can possess. What is captured is not merely a collection of ideas or ideals, it is spiritual chemistry meant to activate and captivate the reader in the most personal way possible."

-- Eldon Marks

"My dear Brother Selwyn, it is a humble honor for me to write this testimonial for you. I was there when The eartHeart Knows was presented to our community; it has become a source of calm, growth; inspiration and insight.

I enjoy it more today as I've grown with your creative and assuring voice. This book is the Genesis that gave birth to your voice among us and for us and more. Thank you; I look forward to more of your writing."

-- Allison Skeete-Hadaway

"Selwyn has always sought to overstand the universal dimensions of interpersonal relationships as he explores the connections between people and the spaces they occupy.

"Be it individually or collectively. He consciously and meticulously explores the boundaries upon which relationships are created, nurtured, sustained, and sometimes dissolved, as well as their impact."

-- Charles A. Monah

From Their Hearts

"A treasure trove of wisdom jam-packed into a space that seems almost inadequate for its purpose. With near-alarming precision the author lays our souls bare as he breaks down each facet of the Life Wheel: our emotional, mental, spiritual, physical, social, behavioral and conscious - each aspect of self handled with an astuteness that fills us with wonder. A worthy reference and a keepsake."

-- Gail Nunes

"The eartHeart Knows is nothing short of inspiring!

Beautifully written the words flow like the songs of angels. It is no ordinary book.

There are few in this world who are gifted with the wisdom, the intuition and drive to produce such a spiritual masterpiece.

There is something in this book for everyone. It has the power to change the course of one's life; to transform and lead one into the awakening. This work came from the Divine. Highly recommended."

-- Mosa Telford

"My brother, thank you for this invaluable gift, 'The eartHeart Knows.' Almost a decade later the reflections are relevant and inspiring. We continue to feast on this smorgasbord of inspirational poems affirming the beauty of 'life.' One luv."

-- Claire Patterson-Monah

The eartHeart Knows Who You Are

"As the author says, this book is a collection of blessings and meditations for one's daily life. I can't add or subtract from that. For me, this book is a comforting piece of art that I pick up when facing life's crossroads.

The book divinely covers "Love", "Peace", "Joy", and "Courage" with an insight that comes from a place of personal passion on the author's part. I met Selwyn in Cape Town several years ago. In person, his demeanor is not far from his writing – full of wisdom, peace, and joyful outbursts.

This is a book that is re-readable, each time with new revelations. It's an ageless masterpiece that keeps on giving."

-- Tendai Jambga

"Selwyn one of my high school friends, emerged from his mundane adolescent and youthful experiences and wove them into a tapestry of testimonies, in the most eloquent, exquisite, profoundly fashioned words, written in his own unique poetic style.

His eartHeart series lay bare his soul and its earthly journeying through the valleys to the mountaintops of his life. Highly recommended for all discerning lovers of poetry and fine writing,"

-- Lady A. Anande Trotman-Joseph

"I am that I am you, but you are not me... - **"The eartHeart Knows."** Son of the earth, full of grace, love, and faith. You are truly the light within the tunnel, the creator of endless opportunities. You are too much to forget. Keep shining my dear friend."

-- Phumi Mngadi - MD NBP Healthcare Solutions SA

From Their Hearts

"The eartHeart Knows is a spiritual masterpiece. This powerful book written by Mr. Selwyn Collins, in his brilliantly fashioned economy of words, will transform your life.

Use a simple 3-step approach to realize its benefits. (1) Reflect on your situation or personal challenge/issue, (2) Guided by your heart, open the book to any page, (3) Meditate on the reading that you were led to open, and the solution will unfold for you."

-- Dr. Sandie Anderson, Independent
Executive Management Consultant

"Selwyn is a once-in-a-lifetime writer whose inimitable style simultaneously illuminates and delights his readers. "The Earth Heart Knows Who You Are," like its predecessor "The Earth Heart Knows," will both center and inspire you. This is a book that everyone should have."

-- Patrick Nicholson

"When Selwyn emerges from his cocoon, expect to be inspired, motivated, and astonished. His metamorphosis is always moved by the ancestors, for Selwyn has learned how to listen and to obey. Selwyn the Vessel.

He speaks about risk, faith, obedience, non-resistance, courage, forgiveness, patience, and love with the poetry and wisdom of all of those who went before us. Listen with your heart and tap in to your own ancestral wisdom."

-- Deborah Rosanwo, M.D.

The eartHeart Knows Who You Are

"Selwyn, what a wonder. Once I opened the book, it was difficult to put it down, so many ahha moments. The reader gets to walk through the doors of your heart. It's like having a conversation with self, seeking and asking the what ifs and finding answers that can only be revealed from a reflective heart.

I appreciate the many encouraging thoughts you shared, the love process of giving praise and allowing gratitude as you salute your parents/family...your blessings and meditations on love, joy, and courage allows one to mediate and start the journey of finding self and revealed truths.

That we all have a purpose, a gift and a light that glows and showcase brilliance, and in your own words, reminds us that 'You are light, radiant and all that is possible'"

-- Sharon Houston

"Selwyn Collins's compelling book "The eartHeart Knows" has been one of the most inspirational and thought-provoking collections to be published by a writer of the Guyanese diaspora.

The release of his new edition is a literary high water mark that's been eagerly awaited for the past 10 years.

Highly recommended reading that is sure to uplift and transform lives for the better."

-- Vince McBean

From Their Hearts

"This book is an elegant mix of Philosophy, Poetry and Inspiration perfectly apportioned by a master "chef" of words to provide a spiritually uplifting menu of thoughts and musings. Thank you my brother for this blessing."

-- John Quintin

"Selwyn's words are from an old spirit deep within. He just has to scratch the surface with his pen, and words of pure joy, introspection, and love flow through the tip.

His words touch the deepest part of our spirits and awaken the love that resides in us all, whether we know it or whether we are capable of it."

-- Dawn S. Walker, Principal DSW:
A Communications Consultancy

"What a writer! What a book! Coming from a technical background, I typically lean towards the consumption of non-fiction books. But no, this one stopped me in my tracks. Unique and different.

The eartHeart Knows pried me open. Disarmed me. Diffused me. Distilled another dimension into my being.

Selwyn Collins writes with such heart and wisdom that as a reader, I felt an internal expansion and transformation as I journeyed across the words and pages. A masterpiece that can only be appreciated if read and internalized."

-- Dr. Rosh Khan

The eartHeart Knows Who You Are

"Selwyn, Your first book 'The eartHeart Knows' is a treasure... You share with your readers that precious part of you that expresses itself with beautiful poetic verses and colorful, creative illustrations.

Reading this book takes you to a level of thinking that is so needed to help us rise to that higher plane of wisdom and enlightenment originally intended for our Humanity. We look forward & joyfully await your second book. Thank you."

-- Monica C. Martin, L.Ac., M.D. Gynaecologist & Acupuncture

"This book brilliantly explores and navigates thought-provoking questions everyone encounters throughout their life journey. It leaves you with little nuggets to help you go beyond your physical-intellectual self. The book provides a fascinating and readable view of mindfulness, leaning into one's authentic self, taking you to the edge, pausing then recalibrating.

It also helps you examine life through spiritual and emotional lenses, which may, at times, highlight your vulnerability. As you read this book, you cannot help but be mindful and intentional with your responses to the path that it takes you on.

The illustrations are helpful and also very effective meditation instruments for better self-awareness and understanding.

I highly recommend it."

-- Lauren Lewis

*Leap if you believe and
believe that you might leap.*

Leap forward in faith, and know that
all things are possible. Trust in the
power of your convictions. You can
achieve anything you set your mind
to. Never give up on your dreams.
Know that with hard work and determination, anything is possible.

CONTENTS

Introduction

The eartHeart Knows Who You Are - Fear is without form, or meaning, unless it eavesdrops the imagination.

*L*ife is an unfolding gift, a divine mystery waiting to be discovered, awakened and embraced. It is time to awaken the divinity within each of us, to accept that we are more than our thoughts and to allow the unfolding of our sacred mystery without question, interruption or judgment. A new dawn is upon us and the world is awakening to a new consciousness, an awareness of a sacred source that gave birth to us all. This same sacred source is needed to give meaning to our lives, to enlighten us with truth and reveal to us the secrets and purpose of being alive.

The universe is awaiting our attention. Her womb, obedient only to our questions, is pregnant with answers, unable to give birth unless we ask.

"Ask and it will be given to you. If you look, you will find. The door will open if you knock."

I have always experienced a deep connection to a divine

The eartHeart Knows Who You Are

and transcendent life. From a young age, I have always been able to sense energy in everything with which I came into contact. With every connection, my environment became an orchard of sensory experiences and mysteries as I questioned everything, from what was nothingness to why women are the only creatures capable of giving birth to another human being. I became fascinated with the divine mystery of the feminine, the magnitude of its responsibility, and the abundant power of being at the core of life itself.

Over time, I became more and more fascinated by the ways that humanity continues to deny the woman her sacred power. While we have become so learned and wise, we have also become more and more disconnected from the sacred core of life. This has led to great suffering on both a personal and a global scale.

Tragically, we must consider the visible effects of our planet's destruction and the less visible inner effects. We must open our hearts and minds to the ways that we are harming ourselves and our world, and find a way to connect with the sacred power within us all.

Today, I am even more curious about why we continue to cut ourselves off from the sacred source that alone can

Introduction

heal, nourish, and transform us. However, I am hopeful because I am optimistic and because the world is awakening to a divine truth that echoes the melodies of time, transcending cultures, geography, and religions.

It should serve as a reminder to all of us that humanity plays an important role in the overall creation and has a responsibility to respect all forms of life. Most importantly, understanding that the feminine and masculine balance is essential to ending suffering. We must find new ways to enlighten and begin the transformation to a balanced humanity in right relationship to spirituality.

I am constantly seeking a better relationship and a fuller experience with the Divine, which is not without challenge. My past experiences are interesting, which often provoke and tempt me with their delightful secrets. The present is innocent and unsuspecting. If I'm not careful, the past can dictate my future. I believe in a life that is free from past interference. A life where even though the past can inform, it cannot dictate how I live.

I believe that life is primarily about relationships, and even more, a quest for happiness. I am confident that happiness is achievable. What this tells me is that life is a journey of learning, exploring, transforming and

The eartHeart Knows Who You Are

experiencing Oneness.

I've been on an even more rigorous journey of self-discovery since 2012, when I wrote "The eartHeart Knows." I am doing my shadow work, praying and meditating more, and practicing deep breathing. I sit still a lot and explore my past traumas to identify the source of my triggers. I am disciplined and obedient to my spirit. I purge my environment, body, mind and spirit, eat and exercise regularly. I'm more intentional in forgiving, giving, loving, and being kind to others.

Something wonderful happened to me. I transformed! I emerged from my cocoon as a much better person. I grew wings. I can fly. This is when I started thinking about all the people who had read "The eartHeart Knows" and how it had helped them. And I realized that there were probably many people out there who could benefit from the book but didn't even know it existed. That's how I decided to write a new book, "The eartHeart Knows Who You Are."

At first, I thought it would be a reprint with some minor changes. Spirit had other plans for me. It is a different book. I've grown in many ways, so it's a more mature book with lots of new observations and insights. Perhaps this too will inspire readers to reflect on their journey and to

Introduction

find their voice along the way.

My objective is not to preach or even teach. It is to invite you to travel with me as I explore some of our emotional hills and valleys. I hope our journey together will help us to understand the human experience and find peace and solace in these troubled times.

Life isn't always easy. Even though there will be many storms that we have to weather, with the right attitude, we can make it through anything and experience some of the hidden treasures in its various lessons.

I am very thankful to the Creator for once again, using me as an instrument to deliver this symphony of thoughts. I ask that you be receptive to the inner wisdom that transcends your intellect and read with an open mind, free of judgment and prejudice. You are unique, so I hope that you'll find within these pages something to make you go deep within and ask thought-provoking questions about yourself and your spirituality.

This book is about belief, commitment, courage, and perseverance. Much more than that, it is about obedience and will. I could not have written this book without these attributes.

The eartHeart Knows Who You Are

For several years, many people who have read the first book have been urging me to write another book like the first. They claimed that my book changed their lives and that it would be a disservice to humanity if I did not write a follow-up.

I was not inspired to write a sequel to 'The eartHeart Knows.' It didn't feel natural. Besides, nothing in me said that I should. All of that changed when I felt an overwhelming urge to share this new phase of my journey. I realized I wanted people to learn from my experiences and new insights. Wisdom had been talking to me again.

This time it was with more urgency. It became increasingly clear that what was in me had to get out and be shared with the world. At first, I thought it was my imagination playing tricks on me until several people from different walks of life approached me with messages about what I must do. Write the book. I became convinced.

I call them, Divine Messengers. Most of them are women, and their message was convincing and urgent. And even though their delivery was different because of their varied backgrounds, they had a common theme. The world is wounded.

Introduction

One person said, "The world is wounded. Many people seem lost and are in pain and suffering and need spiritual guidance and healing."

Another person, sadness in her focused eyes, said, "And you have that message, Selwyn. You are gifted. And you know this. We need to hear that message from you."

Don't wait for permission from the naysayers. Give it to yourself.

It's better to ask for forgiveness than permission because if you fail, people will still respect your effort and admire your courage to try something new and different. However, if we wait for permission, we might never take the risk because we fear failure more than we value success.

The eartHeart Knows Who You Are

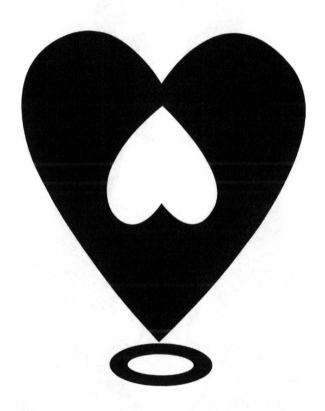

This time, the mirror smiled at me, not with contentment but with acknowledgment. Deep within its reflection, it sees me. It has witnessed my transformation.

If we stop staring so long at the closed door,
we might just notice the one that is opened.

SELWYN A. COLLINS

THE
EartHeart
Knows
WHO YOU ARE

These words are for you, and they are for me.
But not necessarily at the same time.
Take what you need, and leave the rest.

Written & Illustrated
by Selwyn A. Collins

Be still and know that you are much more than an opinion. Know that you're enough.

I Am

I AM THAT. I AM YOU, BUT YOU ARE NOT ME.
IT IS I WHO FOUND YOU AND
AWAITS YOU TO FIND ME.

I Am

Every breath is an opportunity to reinvent yourself and a chance to do something good. You just have to keep pushing forward and believe in yourself!

The eartHeart Knows Who You Are

We all have our crosses to bear in life. Some of us have it worse than others, and w**e all have our struggles**. It's easy to get caught up in our own problems and feel like the world is against us. We need to remember that **our struggles are what make us strong**.

They are what help us grow and learn.

If we can view our struggles as something to be proud of, something that we can overcome, then we will be much better off. **We all have obstacles in our lives** that we need to overcome. And our crosses can help us get across them.

So don't curse the cross you bear. Bear it with pride. Your cross might give you the experience you need to overcome most obstacles.

I Am

*Coincidence is when analysis and logic
try to explain your divinity.*

When The Clouds Won't Drift Away

*I release criticism and expectation.
I am in right action.
I harbor no envy or hate,
I abhor persecution.
I'm here. I'm happy.
I need not hide.
I'm in my sanctuary.
I'm satisfied.
I neither judge nor condemn.
Joy flows freely through me.
I experience love.
I'm in love.
I Am love.*

I Am En.

You found the courage, do you have the will? Can you let go? Do you want to, or would you rather cause pain and suffering, because you believe that you can justify it?

Do not despair if your brilliance or happiness causes some people to leave. Consider that **any light, no matter how small or insignificant, is a threat to darkness**.

No darkness or negativity can survive in its presence.

We are **too magnificent for any label** and too resilient to be altered by anxiety, doubt, people's opinions or fear.

I Am

Lack and loss are just seasons
to the faithful and wise.

The eartHeart Knows Who You Are

Your God-Presence is patient and awaits you to connect. Pray and meditate regularly. **Do whatever your beliefs allow to tune into your quietude.** Prayer, meditation, whatever you use to connect to the quiet within your silence, do it until it becomes as natural as breathing.

It may take a while. So, be patient for all your answers depend on your connecting to Source through your inner quiet. **Whenever you feel the need to be alone it's usually an unconscious desire to connect to the Creator, to be at one.**

When you are in tune you can feel that something. You know this to be true.

I Am

Patience is the best medicine for all wounds. Forgive everyone, but first and foremost forgive yourself.

The eartHeart Knows Who You Are

I am perfect in this moment because this moment is perfect in me.

There is no need to be perfect in order to be happy and fulfilled. All that is required is to be present in the moment and appreciate what is happening right now.

When we are present in the moment, we are free to be ourselves. We are free to express our true nature and love more deeply. As we remain present, we forget about the perfection of others, because our inner light shines brilliantly regardless of anything else.

We can see that everything is exactly as it should be when we're present in this moment. When our minds wander and focus on what we don't have, that's when doubt and fear creep in; but being present does not allow for doubt or fear to exist.

When we appreciate what's happening right now, it's easy for us to let go of the need to control everything. Sometimes life isn't perfect because it's a test—when you experience difficulties, your greatest opportunities lie below them (such as an amazing breakthrough).

I Am

How can my footsteps not be sure
when my heart is pure?

I yearned neither certain knowledge, nor have I
coveted the bosom of wisdom.
Yet I am with understanding.
At times surprising. So thrilling, I dare not
fathom.

I have been told that, some things are better left
unsaid. Why me?
Why keep me quenched and fed?

Am I worthy of manna, of this living bread?
Who will comfort me?
Who will understand this charity?

Who?

The eartHeart Knows Who You Are

When it comes to prayer and meditation, I feel like this is something that I need to share. I'm not perfect, I'm far from it actually, but I do know that there is **power in prayer and meditation**.

I know that when I am still and I pray, I can feel a connection to something much greater than myself. **I feel like I can access wisdom that is beyond me.** I know that when I am still and I meditate, I can feel peace and an unshakeable calmness.

I'm not saying that you should never take action or that you should never try to do things on your own. I'm simply saying that when you are feeling lost, or when you are feeling like you can't do it on your own, **don't be afraid to reach out to a power that is much greater than you**.

Pray, meditate, and be still.

You are never alone.

I Am

The eartHeart Knows Who You Are

*How can I hear you when I am listening to the
symphony of wonderment within me?
How can I love you when love
refuses to make the connection?
How can I deny myself peace?*

*How can you savour the experience
of that you do not understand?
How can I hate that which means nothing to me?*

*How can I restrict the hands of Destiny?
How can I not embrace the sanctity
of the chasm between us?*

How can I choose to be not happy?

I Am En.

I Am

*Be always present, and do not cast your now into
the depths of yesterday's shadows.
Be still and know that you are a gift.
You are magnificent.*

You feel it's time to connect with your inner self more strongly, to follow your intuition and do what feels right, in order to achieve your deepest desires. Even though your resistance is weakening, it's still there. Is this due to a lack of balance, or destiny?

Perhaps it is neither. The mind is a powerful thing, and is always seeking to control and manipulate us into doing what it wants. It is a master at deception, convincing us that what it wants is in our best interest. All too often, we allow our minds to get the better of us. We dwell on the past, worry about the future, and fear the present.

The mind is a powerful tool, and it is also a dangerous one. We need to be aware of its tricks and learn to control it, rather than letting it control us.

The eartHeart Knows Who You Are

Perhaps the silence within challenges our confidence and dares us to leap into the unknown. Our treasures might also be right there, hidden, awaiting.

I Am, I Am light, I Am All Right

Forsake me not my comfort
Heal my wounds, calm my hurt.
My heart is heavy.
Grey clouds descend on me, mountains rumble.
I'm still in my temples.
I must find my will, I must not stumble.
Persistent thoughts, dark and foreboding,
They conspire to test my faith.
I'm patient, I pray, and I meditate.
I'll win this battle. I await.
This thing cannot defeat me,
I am too gifted.
I am light.
I Am En!

I Am

*Accept no, because yes is infinitely jealous
and will soon follow.*

So, you fell. It is true that the fear of what others think or say about you may be paralysing and even more painful than the pain from the actual fall. Know that if you can weather and survive the emotional and psychological storm, then what can you not achieve?

What shore is beyond your reach? Really?

The eartHeart Knows Who You Are

If you ever feel that you have hit rock bottom, know that this is just the moment before your ascent. New life always sprouts after winter.

It's easy to feel like you've hit rock bottom when life gets tough. Maybe you've lost your job, or your relationship is falling apart. Maybe you're struggling with your mental health, or you're just feeling lost and alone. Whatever the reason, it can be tough to see past the pain and believe that things will get better.

It's important to **remember that rock bottom is just a moment** - a point in time that you will eventually move past. Just like winter always gives way to spring, there is always hope for a better tomorrow.

So if you're feeling lost and alone, know that you're not alone. And know that better days are on the horizon.

Do not despair. Believe in yourself, have faith, and know that all will be well because all is well.

I Am

If you have faith and truly believe, why pray and ask for the same thing more than once?

The eartHeart Knows Who You Are

May each breath you take be a breath of rejuvenation.
May each moment, be a moment of satisfaction.
May each ray of light, be a ray of hope and inspiration.

With each breath, feel the light of the universe coursing through your veins, illuminating your darkness. Feel it cleansing you, purifying you, and restoring your peace, your happiness.

There is nothing more important than your breath: and no moment more important than this moment.

There is no one more important than you.

No one.

I Am

The power of what happened to you is not in your thoughts. It is in your reaction to them.

Whatever our beliefs, **we know when something doesn't feel right within us** or in our surroundings. It could be the energy we feel, the intuition we get or just the overall spirit we sense. Even though we may not be aware of what it is, we can feel it nonetheless.

This is what we call our sixth sense. It is that thing that allows us to see beyond what is physically present. It is what allows us to feel the presence of something else, even if we cannot see it. **Some people are more in tune with their sixth sense than others**. We all have it to some degree. And, we can all learn to develop it further.

When your pores or the hairs at the back of your neck raise, you think of someone and they show up or call, the thing you keep thinking you don't want to happen, does. Our intuition is our innate guidance system, designed to keep us safe and help us make the best choices.

It is our inner knowing, and it is always trying to guide us to what is best for us.

I Am

The answer you seek may be in
your openness to a new idea.

No matter how dull or dark the situation is, let's live the best we can with what we have, even if we think it's nothing, for life is the greatest something.

We all have our ups and downs, our light moments and our dark moments. But no matter how dark or dull the situation is, let's try to live the best we can with what we have. Because even if we think we have nothing, life itself is the greatest something.

Sure, there will be times when we feel like we have nothing to live for. But even in those moments, let's remember that we always have life itself. And as long as we have life, we have the potential for happiness and joy.

So no matter how dark or dull the situation is, let's try to make the best of it. **Let's live our lives to the fullest, even if we think we have nothing**. Because in reality, we have the greatest something – life itself.

The eartHeart Knows Who You Are

Who are you to allow your doubts, inhibitions, and failures to prevent you from achieving your goals and reaching your potential?

Furthermore, **who are you to deprive the rest of us of the chance to experience your greatness?**

The **enemy knows your weaknesses** and will use them against you. They may reveal your secrets, find and expose your hidden skeletons, attack your finances, and use those closest to you to hurt you.

Do not underestimate your enemy. They will not hesitate to use pain, procrastination, and addiction against you. **Fight wisely**, and do not go into battle alone.

I Am

I have come to believe that jealousy is not possible without admiration.

Pray for covering and discernment and be watchful. Know that those closest to you can be unwitting pawns against you especially when their state of mind or the condition of their hearts avails them to be used.

I have come to believe that more than perfection, we seek reasons not to accept what is as it is.

When your confidence threatens others, do not expect kindness or understanding. They may be motivated to tear you down so they can feel comfortable. Be strong and claim your space. Do not be intimidated.

Ugliness will eventually reveal itself no matter how well it disguises itself because either beauty or goodness compels it to be free.

I Am

Do we have the capacity to love our enemies as we love ourselves? Do we ever really try? Do we even ever want to?

What if loving our enemies as ourselves is only part of the story; and what if the greatest secret never told is that loving them is the most powerful connection to our higher self?

What if our enemies were created as carriers of our keys, our missing links to true greatness?

Why were some of them friends before enemies; and why did they come into our lives?
Why such powerful connections, and though negative, are they really connections, or are they just interpretations?

Why do thoughts of some of them evoke such strong emotions?
Why such powerful reactions?
Why so much energy?

The eartHeart Knows Who You Are

What if loving our enemies as ourselves is the key to awaking the Christ in all of us? Just asking ...

I Am

*Every moment is an opportunity to reinvent
yourself, so be generous.*

The eartHeart Knows Who You Are

It was around midnight when the questions came with the ferocity of a violent storm, faster than I could answer, then this,

"Have you walked every step in their shoes and have they in yours...?"

I answered and with the suddenness of a moment, the storm passed. In its wake, clarity, contentment, peace.

The enemy will try to douse your light because they can see your brilliance. They can see your greatness before you. Do not fear them, for even those close to you are powerless when you believe and are aware of your God-Presence. You are a powerful being, created in the image and likeness of God. You have within you everything you need to fulfill your destiny.

When you remember and accept who you are, the enemy's attempts to bring you down will fail.

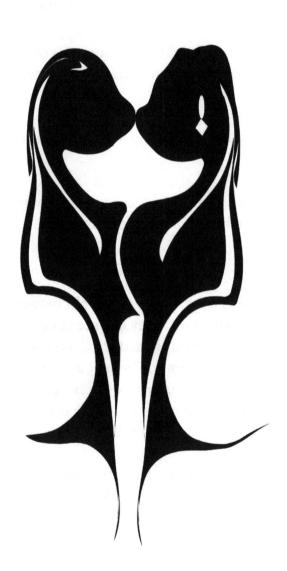

LOVE

Love is abundant in me for
I have come here to love,
and to be in love.

Love

Oh storms, teach me your secrets.
I promise not to tell.

Beyond the anger and other negativity, his primary challenge is to see his lover's beauty where others fail.

Her Beauty.

It's easy to get caught up in the negative aspects of our lives and the people in them. We see the anger, the hurt, the frustration, and we forget about the good. The beauty.

For one man, beyond the anger and other negativity, his primary challenge is to see his lover's beauty where others fail.

When they first met, he was immediately drawn to her fiery spirit. She was passionate about life and everything in it. Her zest for life was contagious and he found himself falling head over heels in love with her.

However, over time, he started to see the negative aspects of her personality more and more. The anger. The frustration. It was like she was a completely different person than the one he had fallen in love with.

But he still loved her. He knew that beneath all of the anger and negativity, there was still the same beautiful woman he had fallen in love with.

And so, his primary challenge became to see her beauty, even when others couldn't. To see the good in her, even when it was hidden beneath the bad.

It hasn't been easy, but it's worth it. Because when he looks at her, he doesn't see the negative aspects of her personality. He sees the beautiful woman he fell in love with.

And that's all that matters.

Love

Your desire for others to be happy stimulates your own happiness.

It is not passionate love that most frightens us or robs us of our confidence. It is when we realize that it is not possible without absolute surrender.

The eartHeart Knows Who You Are

We can heal ourselves by healing others. It's a simple concept, really. When we help others, we're also helping ourselves. It's a win-win situation.

Why? Because when we give of ourselves, we're tapping into a reservoir of love that is within us. And that love is healing. It's like a balm that soothes our wounds and helps us to feel whole again.

Wish others well and mean it; suppress the urge to cause others pain; pay a compliment and mean it; apologize and really mean it, then behold the wonderment from within as calmness surrenders to you.

When we take the time to reach out to others, to help them heal their wounds, we find that our own wounds begin to heal as well.

Love

The heart awaits your love
that it might beat divine rhythms.

It's easy to be judgemental. We all do it, whether we realize it or not. It's human nature to judge others based on our own experiences, pain and suffering.

What if you realize that you're being judgemental to a friend based on these reasons?

Do you have the courage to apologize, stop playing games, and accept responsibility? Or will you find a way to blame them for your actions?

Resistance to what is or denying what happened when you know it did, interrupts the flow and causes disharmony, dis-ease, sorrow, or lack.

The eartHeart Knows Who You Are

In your heart you know when someone is right for you. But one of the things that can often rob us of our confidence in love is the fear that we will not be able to surrender ourselves completely. This fear can prevent us from ever really giving ourselves over to the experience of love.

However, it is important to remember that surrender is not something that should be feared. Instead, it should be seen as an opportunity to fully experience the depths of love.

When we are able to let go of our fears and surrender ourselves to love, we will find that we are able to achieve a much deeper level of connection with our partner.

This connection will be built on trust, respect, and a true understanding of one another. It is only when we are able to achieve this level of connection that we will be able to truly experience the passion and fire of love.

Love

*Be the lover you seek and your lover
will find you.*

When it comes to love, we often think that we need to find the right person. We go on dates, we swipe right, we hope and pray that we'll find that one special someone. But what if the key to finding love is actually being the right person?

It sounds simple, but it's true. Be the lover you seek and your lover will find you. If you're looking for someone who is kind, caring, and loving, then be those things yourself. Be the person who you would want to date, and eventually, you will find someone who feels the same way about you.

It's not always easy to be the best version of ourselves, but it's worth it. When we show our best selves to the world, we attract people who are also their best selves. So if you're ready to find true love, start by being the best lover you can be.

The eartHeart Knows Who You Are

The night is hushed, but restless.
She cannot sleep for the past is boastful with
secrets it's condemned to keep.
The dawn is early, but trapped in a spell by an
impetuous past with much to tell.

Love

So he said to his lover ...

You see weakness, My Darling, but I see strength in my unconditional love for you. You see a person who is not perfect, who makes mistakes, and who is sometimes weak. You see someone who is not always strong, who is sometimes fearful and who sometimes falters.

But what you don't see is the strength that lies within me - the strength to love you unconditionally, no matter what.

You see, when I look at you, I don't see your flaws and weaknesses. I see the beauty and perfection that is YOU. I see the person who I love with all my heart, and who I know I will love forever.

I see the strength of your character, even when you are at your weakest. I see the courage you show, even when you are afraid. I see the determination you have, even when you feel like giving up.

These are the things that I see when I look at you. And they are the things that I love about you. I may not always be perfect, but I will always love you perfectly.

The eartHeart Knows Who You Are

I am not dedicated to you loving me. I am dedicated to you being greater than you were yesterday.

A rose does not hide its beauty because you were too busy to notice it the last time you passed. And a tree does not forsake its fruits because a storm destroyed them before they were ready for harvest.

Nature has a way of continuing on, no matter what obstacles are in its way. And, just like nature, we should not give up on ourselves when we face difficult times.

We all have storms in our lives that can damage or destroy what we've built. If we are like the rose or the tree, we will not let those storms defeat us. We will continue to grow and thrive, despite the challenges we face.

You can get through anything life throws your way.

Love

True love is honest, pure,
and a great source of energy.

Manage your spiritual health by accepting the present. Accept this moment. Your source of pain is in your preoccupation with the past and the future.

Even if you don't believe in the NOW, assume that NOW is where possibilities happen, and it is all you have. Then say yes to this moment.

Why create resistance to something that already is? Empower yourself and say 'yes' to life, then behold how life starts rewarding rather than rejecting you.

Beware the power of illness and loss to condemn you to doubt, hate, and misery.

The eartHeart Knows Who You Are

Love flows through you and you are created with divine love, so love the way you desire to love, and the way you know that you must love.

Be your magnificence and do not change who you are because they didn't love you as passionately, or as authentically as you loved them, and opted out rather than reciprocated.

Know that you are rare and valuable, There is only one you. There is only one of you. You are one-of-a-kind with your unique talents, passions, and purpose.

You were created to stand out from the crowd, to shine brightly in this world. You are here for a reason, and that reason is to make a difference.

You have the power to change lives, to touch hearts, and to make the world a better place. So never doubt your worth or your ability to make a positive impact.

You are rare and gifted, and the world needs you.

Love

*Who questions depth of love
when two hearts trust each other?*

The eartHeart Knows Who You Are

If you are in love and willing to give your heart, and you don't because of your history, then know that you are held hostage by fear and the tyranny of your past.

It's hard to move on from a past that haunts us. It's even harder to open ourselves up to love again when someone has hurt us. However, if we don't let go of our fear, we'll never be able to experience the beauty and joy that love can bring.

Yes, giving our hearts can be scary. It's also quite rewarding. When we're able to let go of our fear and give ourselves to someone, we can experience a kind of love that is truly beautiful.

So if you're in love and afraid to give your heart, know it's time to let go of your fear and give yourself a chance.

Love

Love someone unconditionally today,
even if it's you.

Love is a divine flow we cannot control. It is admirable, awesome, brilliant, wonderful, and can be intoxicating. However, loving is love in action. Love is forgiving. Love is healing. Love is nurturing. Love is strengthening.

Loving is humanity in bliss, and a covenant with your spirituality.

Love the new stranger until you understand them, then be loving without inhibitions.

That stranger can be you...

The eartHeart Knows Who You Are

𝔜our desire for others to have more, connects you to the source of abundance and invokes unlimited possibilities in your life.

Love

Humility is kneeling at the well to drink and not expecting it to rise to meet you.

Be free to flow as you were created to flow. Be genuine and embrace you. Do not ignore, censor or resist what is happening within. Even though it is written we were created perfect, we must continue to evolve; to strive for a better version of yourselves.

An enlightening and powerful journey begins when we reach beyond ourselves, find our truth, embrace it and open ourselves to the unknown.

This journey is not always easy. There will be times when we will want to give up. If we persevere, we will find that the rewards are more than worth the effort.

Know that even though the first step begins a journey, it is the next step that completes it.

The eartHeart Knows Who You Are

Can you think of those moments when you were so excited, so confident, so filled with euphoria that nothing and no one could get close enough to disturb you?

When no negativity or inequity, no persistent memory of mistakes and unfinished endeavors, no knowledge of your imperfections, and no enemy could render you hopeless and helpless?

Recapture the essence of those special moments and know within your heart that nothing can corrupt your equilibrium, nothing can shackle you. Not even your limitations.

Love

You can succeed at the improbable if you awake early, before doubt, before your limitations, and much earlier than your reality.

When I was younger, I used to believe that if I wanted something badly enough, I could make it happen. I was naïve and optimistic and I thought that if I just put my mind to it, I could achieve anything. I believed that I could succeed at the improbable.

Now, I'm not so naïve. I know that it takes more than just desire to achieve something. It takes hard work, dedication, and determination.

But I still believe in the power of the mind. I still believe that if we set our sights on something and put our all into it, we can achieve the impossible.

Believe in yourself and your ability to achieve the improbable. Wake up early and start working towards your dreams. Don't let doubt or reality stop you. You can achieve the improbable if you believe in yourself and are willing to work hard for it.

The eartHeart Knows Who You Are

How Can I Not Be Grateful?

I surrender to my awakening,
my transformation, my salvation.
The Creator made me as I am, and I am grateful.
My cup is full.
I am a gift and gifted.
I create with abandon and without caution.
I am light. I shine without permission.
I give without conditions, forgive without reason,
and love without inhibitions.

I am in the bosom of forgiveness.
I accept it as it is, then see it for what it is.
I forgave myself. I've forgiven you.
Now, I'm in bliss. I'm in ecstasy.
Joy is abundant and sets me free.
I am present, and the present.
I am the gift at this moment.

I Am En.

Love

Be not afraid to shine, for anyone without envy or jealousy can withstand your brilliance.

You my friend, got this. You forgave yourself and the unforgiven, created and innovated without much, healed a broken heart, and empowered the forsaken.
And as if that wasn't enough ...
You survived storms, precipices, and chasms.
You worked tirelessly to release the better you, survived doubts, fears, and inhibitions. Conquered your insecurities, and sat at the tables of your enemies.

You exercise, introspect, meditate, pray, and purge regularly. You give and love unconditionally.

NOW, you ponder what?
Fear who?
How is it possible for any enemy to defeat this bolder, boundless, brighter you?
How can anyone?
Who dares to try?

I Am En

The eartHeart Knows Who You Are

WHAT IF YOU HAD LIMITED BREATHS?

When we're tempted to hate or resent someone, we must consider how many more breaths we have before our last. Is there enough to spend on hurting someone, a relative, or a friend? Is there enough time to fight against envy, jealousy, hate, or false testimonies?

We live in a world that is constantly trying to tear us down. To make us believe that we are not good enough, that we are not worthy of love or respect. It's easy to give in to those negative voices and start to hate and resent those around us.

Before we do, we must remember that we are not promised tomorrow. That the time we have is limited and we should spend it wisely.

Hate and resentment are two of the most destructive emotions we can feel. They take up valuable space in our hearts and minds that could be used for so much more. If we could only let go of those negative feelings, we would be so much happier and our lives would be so much richer.

Sure, there will be times when someone does something to hurt us. We have to remember that they're not worth our hatred or resentment. We must move on and focus on the good in our lives. We all make mistakes. We're human. We must learn from our mistakes and move on. Life is too short to dwell on the past.

If you're feeling tempted to hate or resent someone, remember how many more breaths you have before your last. Is it worth it to spend your time on earth hating or resenting someone? Or, would you rather focus on the positive and enjoy the time you have with your loved ones?

Is there enough?

You decide.

The eartHeart Knows Who You Are

Love as you were created to love. At least indulge the splendor of the experience.

No matter the outcome, we should never regret love. Love is a beautiful thing and we should be grateful for all the happiness and joy that it brings into our lives, even if it doesn't last forever.

Just like a basket can't hold water, we are powerless to stop love in all her glory and majesty when she seeps into our pores.

Even though we may not be able to control how love unfolds in our lives, we can control how we react to it.

So next time you find yourself in the midst of love, don't be afraid to embrace it, even if you don't know how it will all turn out.

In the end, love is always worth the risk.

Love

I asked love to have mercy upon me for contentment has made me vulnerable.

If I may indulge you, my dear. I ask that you have mercy on me as I am recklessly in love with you. I crave your bosom, my darling. I am addicted.

I might succumb to my vulnerabilities. Please be merciful!

The eartHeart Knows Who You Are

Love hummed a soft melody,
"*I am only possible when you are vulnerable, and it is only through your vulnerability that you can experience the true wonderment of me...*"
"*My dearest Love, you cause such deep and searing pain! How can I trust you? Why should I?*"

"*Many have accused me of suffering, though I am pure and delightful. I cause joy, never pain.*

"*I am the light in the dark, the hope in the hopeless. I am the love that endures, even when all else fails.*

"*I am love.*"

Love

*Romance has a flavour
the selfish will never taste.*

The eartHeart Knows Who You Are

When you love someone and know they love you, be patient with them.

It's so easy to get caught up in the heat of the moment and want everything to happen immediately. We live in a fast-paced world where we're constantly inundated with instant gratification, so it's no wonder that we often expect the same from our relationships.

However, when it comes to love, it's important to remember that good things come to those who wait. If you're in a relationship with someone you love and you know that they love you back, be patient with them.

Be slow to anger, especially about the small stuff. It is possible that either of you might not be in equilibrium or the two of you might be out of sync.

Love

Help others recognize their treasures within and you'll discover yours.

Even though the separation from something or someone you love can be excruciating, it is usually the only key to growth, survival, transformation, and wisdom.

Love abundantly and passionately from your heart. Do not listen to the Mind or the Ego. They are prejudiced and way too selfish to love unconditionally.

FORGIVE THEM

Forgiveness reboots the heart and also nourishes, strengthens, and sustains it.

When we forgive someone, we are choosing to release the hurt and anger we feel. This can be incredibly difficult, especially if the person who hurt us is someone close to us.

However, forgiveness is important because it allows us to move on from the pain. It allows us to heal and to rebuild our relationships.

Forgiveness is not easy. It takes time, effort, and patience. It is worth it.

Love

You have to be brave to love unconditionally, because true love comes from being able to forgive ourselves and our enemies.

Participate in the rhythm of abundance by giving to empty your cup so you might create space to receive and give again.

We've all been there. You're so busy filling up your cup with all life's obligations and commitments that you don't have time for anything else. **What happens when your cup starts spilling over?** You can't enjoy the things you love because you're too busy trying to keep everything together.

It's important to remember that a cup is most useful when it's empty. Try not to let your cup get so filled that it spills over. **Make time for yourself and your passions**, which is the only way to avoid burnout and keep your cup running smoothly.

The eartHeart Knows Who You Are

𝔉ree your mind.
Calm your nerves and try to relax.
Breathe. Let it go so that you might tap into the field
of possibility. You create whatever you are constantly
thinking and worrying about.
Be thankful, be grateful, be kind, be still.
Forgive yourself and them.
Eat right.

Purge your environment, body, mind, and spirit.

Detox. Ground. Drink lots of water.
Exercise, pray, and meditate regularly.
Let go, it and them.
Be present.
Deny doubt.
Ignore the past, so that you might forget you can't
and realize that you can.

I Am En.

PEACE

IF I HAD TWO LIVES I WOULD FORSAKE THE ONE
THAT REALLY OFFENDS YOU, THEN I WOULD LIVE
THE OTHER AS IF IT WERE THE ONLY ONE.

Peace

Do not empower the enemies with your reaction. You are who you think you are, and not what they say you are.

If you're always focused on the end result, you'll never enjoy the present moment, and will miss out on the richness of the journey.

When your spirit doesn't feel right about some-one, pay attention. It is being disturbed. Find a way to still your mind and tune in to your inner self. Listen to what your intuition is telling you, believe, and act accordingly.

The eartHeart Knows Who You Are

Be calm and maintain your equilibrium even when the turbulence frightens you. A balanced ship can survive any storm.

It's easy to get caught up in what other people think of us. We can start to believe the negative things they say and doubt our own worth. But it's important to remember that **we are not defined by other people's opinions.**

We are who we think we are. And we should never give our power away by letting someone else control our thoughts and emotions.

Peace

*Peace should not be a challenge
but an obsession!*

The challenge is not in knowing you must evolve. It is in believing that it's your divine obligation.

The eartHeart Knows Who You Are

The tree said to the violent wind, "*I will neither allow you to trick me into fighting you, nor corrupt my inner peace. You cannot move me for I have chosen the path of no resistance.*"

To be overwhelmed is human. Even though it reminds us of our weaknesses, we should also remember that we have the power to **change the changeable things**.

When we change our vocabulary and change our perspectives, the universe responds in a way that everything around us adjusts to the new us.

As it is written, "Ask and you will receive." The universe will give us what we desire.

In spite of this, we must believe and be vigilant, because our gifts may not arrive in a package we recognize.

Peace

Guard your moments for they are
bread crumbs to your happiness.

You just heard something that may not be the truth. You are furious, your heart races, your blood pressure rises, and you want to cuss. There is no reasoning with you.

So ...

What just happened?
What really changed?
What if you hadn't heard it?
What if you don't really care?
Who or what is really in control?

The eartHeart Knows Who You Are

This moment is your moment. You are the present and a divine gift. You are the light darkness dreads, so step out of the way and let your inner light shine.

Even though you may be a small lamp in a large room and sometimes the only lamp. When the darkness is closing in, realize that even though you may be a small lamp, you are still light.

Darkness is not permitted to consume you because you are light.

Remember who you are.

I've come to believe that forgiveness is just the beginning of freedom and power, for it only prepares the soil. The harvest is in forgetting and forgiving. Perhaps it is why so many of us never reap.

Peace

Be patient - healing takes time.

The eartHeart Knows Who You Are

You are a light, obligated to shine your brightest without fear of consequences. Those who envy you because they cannot stand your brilliance will seek cover or leave.

It's a simple message, and one that we all need to hear from time to time.

We live in a world that can be dark and cold, and it's easy to forget our own light in the midst of it all. We have to remember that we are obligated to shine our brightest, no matter what.

Those who envy us because they can't stand our brilliance will seek cover or leave. They might try to bring us down. We cannot let them. We have to keep shining, no matter what.

It's not always easy. We owe it to ourselves and to the world to be the best that we can be. So keep shining, no matter what.

Peace

Peace should not be a challenge.
It should be an obsession!

Those who invest in being right or having the last word are never in the market for peace.

They are usually the ones who are quick to anger and slow to forgive. They hold grudges, look for fights, talk a lot, and hardly listen.

If you find yourself in a disagreement with someone, ask yourself if you're more interested in being right or in having peace. If it's the latter, then take a step back, take a deep breath, and try to see the situation from the other person's perspective.

You might be surprised at how much more peaceful your relationships will become.

What most people seek and value the most is **freedom**. And to them, freedom is **peace of mind**.

Peace

I discovered the friend in friendship.

The eartHeart Knows Who You Are

I was I was at a crossroads in my life, not knowing which way to turn next, when peace spoke to me. Its tone was urgent, solemn as it said, "Must you be stubborn without reason? Must you even be stubborn? If you must, can you not have your way without rejecting me?"

I nodded, hesitant.

"I am here for you. Let me in," Peace continued. "I cannot force my way upon you. Acknowledge my presence. Indulge me. Taste my essence. My gentleness will caress and comfort you, but you must accept me and invite me in for such intimacy."

This message gave me the strength to take the next step forward, even though I was unsure and reluctant at first. And I am glad I did, because peace has brought new comfort and understanding into my life.

Peace

Bid me not against my nature for I am that I am, Peace.
Remember I exist.

Peaceful is when what it is or isn't ceases to matter.

In your meditation, in the comforts of your belief, deep within your quietude, beyond the shadows of your aloneness and the frequency of your silence, you are in the bosom of your sanctuary.

Peace is possible with each breath. As you inhale, its fragrance seeps into you and frees you from your anxieties, doubts, and fears. Your conscience is free. You are free.

You are at one, so you must not ponder the unknown. Know that in this space, at this moment, nothing can disturb you, harm you, or deny your will.

Peace

Only you can decide whether the taste of freedom is worth more than the pain from the sacrifice.

Everything eventually changes, so nothing is permanent. The strongest storm eventually dissipates.

A good captain knows this. She is a woman who understands the power of the storm. She is not afraid of it. She respects its strength.

She knows that her strength and resourcefulness will see her through any storm. She is patient and wise.

She's goes with the flow.

THE PRESENT

All that is me, is in you, yet you lust the past.
Indulge me, I need you for I am selfish.
The Past is cunning and unjust.
Crave not her bosom
Her milk is dry, bitter, of dust.

Embrace me that you might be free.
Seek me, for I am laden with possibilities.
Stay with me, I crave your attention.
Get to know me for I am your salvation.

Converse with me, indulge my wisdom.
Rest with me, claim my bosom
Gorge my milk, taste my freedom.
Embrace me, for I am your light, your way, and
your gift.

I am the presence and your gift in this moment.
I Am En.

Peace

After all the excuses have taken their place
I'm still responsible.

I am and so it is

I am in obedience.
Deep within my silence.
I am in meditation, absolute and content.
I am way beyond doubt or anxiety.
Quietude is within and upon me.

I covenant with peace. I need not worry.
I am that I am what I must be.
Abundant questions, deep and probing.
I am introspective, listening.

I believe in love and forgiveness.
I observe without expectations or prejudice.
I seek no vengeance or retribution.
I am in salvation.

I am in sanctuary for I realize that everything is as
it is supposed to be.

Peace

How could my footsteps not be sure if my mind is pure?

If the enemy (negative energy) seems close to conquering you, remember that you have the power to deny it victory by **being present and reclaiming your moment**.

If you're feeling angry, take a deep breath and ask yourself why. If the reason for your anger is **a friend or someone who is usually kind and respectful**, it's likely that the enemy is present.

If it's an object of your desire, something you really want, then **postpone your gratification** by detaching from it.

The eartHeart Knows Who You Are

When you're under attack, try to stay calm and think clearly. In most cases, the attacker is more motivated by their own problems than by anything you've done.

Peace

Forgive and understand the person on the other end of the argument and peace will find its way to you.

We all know that feeling when we're finally home after a long day. The door closes behind us and we exhale a deep breath of relief. Everything feels better when we're in our own space - the comfort of our own bed, the peace of being surrounded by our favorite things.

It's important to remember that our environment has a big impact on our mood and overall well-being. If we're constantly surrounded by chaos and negativity, it's going to start taking a toll on us. On the other hand, if we **surround ourselves with things that bring us peace of mind and lift our spirits**, we'll feel so much better.

Think about it - when you walk into a room that's full of light and happiness, doesn't it just make you feel good? We should strive to create that feeling in our own homes. **Fill your space with things that make you happy**. Hang up some posters or photos that make you smile. Put out some flowers or candles that make the room smell nice.

It's also important to declutter and get rid of anything that's weighing you down. If there's something in your home that's constantly causing you stress, get rid of it! **Life is too short to be surrounded by negativity**.

Take some time to create a space that you love. Surround yourself with things that bring you peace of mind and lift your spirit.

You'll be so glad you did.

Change your perspective and change your reality.

Peace

Never are you more prepared to be filled with peace than when you forgive the unforgivable.

When vengeance dominates the moment and you are overwhelmed, peace will find you if you can just say thank you for the experience and move on.

It's easy to let our emotions take over. We can become so wrapped up in our own anger and pain that we can't see anything else. But if we can **take a step back and be grateful for the experience**, even if it wasn't what we wanted, we can find peace.

It's not always easy to do, but it's so important. When we're consumed by our own emotions, we're not able to see clearly. We can't make wise decisions or see the good in people and situations. But when we're at peace, we can see things more clearly and make better choices.

If you're struggling to forgive someone, it's okay to seek help from a therapist or counselor. They can help you work through the emotions you're feeling and help you find a way to move on.

It's important to take care of yourself after you've been hurt. Make sure you're getting enough rest, eating healthy, and spending time with supportive people.

These things will help you **heal and eventually find peace.**

Peace

A kind word or act of kindness can change someone's life, maybe even yours.

Give back. The world needs healing. You can **make a difference** with one kind gesture.

Be merciful. Mercy is the process of braking, turning the wheel, changing direction and discovering **you** in the center of your chaos.

Mercy is the key to **restoring your equilibrium** and peace. It also protects and sustains your harmony, your happiness and the energy you would otherwise lose to vengeance.

Give without conditions even if you cannot see the results.

Peace

An authentic and unconditional giver
seldom waits to be asked.

Don't underestimate karma. It's the unspoken consequence of fate that will always come back to you, whether good or bad.

Many people believe karma is fair and always gives us what we deserve. Many believe that even if you're sorry or apologize, you can't stop it from happening.

Karma is like the rain or the wind—it doesn't care who you are, so it is unwise to take action without considering the consequences of your decisions..

The eartHeart Knows Who You Are

Don't let anyone steal your desire, your joy, or your laughter. They are the keys to your longevity and the spells that conjure contentment, happiness, and success.

Peace

A sincere apology may not neutralize the pain.
However, it can start the healing process.

Sometimes it can be difficult to imagine that the ones who are causing pain can also be in pain. **Deep pain can manifest in strange ways**.

Vengeance prevents us from achieving inner peace. It's like ink - once you get it on you, it's hard to get rid of. Loving your enemies is not a kindness extended to them. It is a way of taking care of yourself, allowing you to grow and develop spiritually.

Any talk of peace is meaningless without your heart's permission. True peace begins within your heart, so speaking the word is without its true essence if your heart is not invested.

When your heart is at peace, that's when you can really start to make a difference in the world. You can start to create change from a place of love and compassion, rather than from a place of anger and hatred.

Most people will agree that **change involves discomfort**. However, this is only true if you refuse to change. Over time, **refusing to change will always more painful**.

JOY

WORLDLY RICHES MAY POINT US IN THE
DIRECTION OF HAPPINESS, BUT ONLY THE JOY OF
BEING CAN GUARANTEE AND SUSTAIN IT.

Joy

It is not the gift. It's your perception of the gift that determines its value.

The moment you choose to have but not to possess, to receive but not to accumulate, and to be in control but not controlling, you awaken happiness and kindle the flame of joy.

You may have heard it said that happiness is a choice. And while that may be true to some extent, there's more to it than simply making a decision to be happy.

True happiness comes from a place of balance. It's about learning to accept life as it is and to find joy in the simple things.

It's about being present in the moment and savoring the good moments, while also being able to let go of the bad.

It's about being grateful for what you have, while also

being open to receiving more.

It's about having enough self-awareness to know when you're out of balance and need to make a change.

And it's about learning to trust yourself and your own intuition.

When you're able to find this balance, happiness will naturally follow. If you're ready to start on the path to true happiness, remember that it starts with a choice.

Choose to have, but not to possess. Choose to receive, but not to accumulate. Choose to be in control, but not controlling, and you'll be well on your way to a more joyful life.

Smile and let go.

Joy

Things might not be perfect, but that doesn't mean you can't enjoy your moments. Smile until your heart welcomes happiness.

The eartHeart Knows Who You Are

Smile, even when you're feeling troubled.
Smile, when you're feeling lonely and though the
pain is unbearable.
Smile, even when you think it's impossible.
Smile until your heart is stable.
Smile so happiness will get the signal.
Smile, even when you're hurting from a fall.
Just smile.

Happiness is an incredibly powerful force. It's like a magical elixir that can make us feel more energetic and motivated. It can comfort, heal, nurture, and restore us. **Happiness is our internal compass** to peace, love, good health, and abundance.

Consider it most valuable and to be cherished. It is our internal fountain of youth, so guard it against anger, self-doubt, and irrational fear.

Be happy. It's your birthright.

Joy

Envy is the unconscious form of praise.

I am in obedience
I am in love
I surrender to this gift
I am in divine presence
I am in bliss and grateful
I am in abundance, my cup is full
I surrender to obedience
I seek no understanding or evidence
I am at peace within my silence
I Am En

The eartHeart Knows Who You Are

Giving awakens the abundance in joy.

A cup is most useful when empty, so give when it's full that it might be empty to be refilled.

Never allow your cup to become so full that it has no room for receiving. Instead, make space for new and exciting things to come into your life.

It's a new day and a new opportunity to start fresh. Today is the day to operate from a space of abundance and **empty your cup so that you can fill it up with new, wonderful things**.

Your heart will rejoice in gladness that you did.

Give so that you may receive, and receive so that you may give. This is the **rhythm of abundance**.

Joy

I forsake the past because its importance is of no consequence to me.

The eartHeart Knows Who You Are

I have sanitized my imagination and exorcised my demons. Broken shackles of contemplation and opinion. Now, fear is without claim or dominion.

Pity, an impetuous flaw in the tapestry of love, is now the last speck within reach of a cleansing joy.

Persistence finds relief in an accepting heart. Curiosity is damned yet craves to know this mysterious power that is love.

Arrogance covets recognition as it pretends to be humble.

Vengeance falls from grace to know its place. Peace is safe from anxiety.

Safe in the bosom of my eternal fast, I'm free from the thirst of a tyrannical past.

Joy

Of course, you can have it all. Well, are you prepared to give up everything?

I'm calm within my reflection
I know no fear or inhibition

My will has a new function
I am without anxiety or worry

Peace has found me
I am in glee
No darkness can consume me
I am free

The eartHeart Knows Who You Are

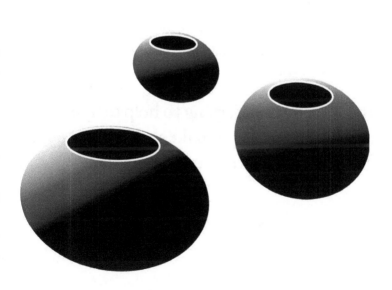

Joy

Forgive yourself and give your heart some time.
Joy is patient.

Why waste time and energy blaming others for not understanding you when you can take the time to understand them?

It can be very satisfying to help others, even in small ways. It all makes a difference and can really brighten someone's day.

The eartHeart Knows Who You Are

You are beautiful, inside and out, and it is
through you that joy
reminds us of its eloquence.

Joy

Be genuinely happy for others and happiness will never be too far from you.

If there's one thing that life has taught me it's that happiness is a choice. Happiness is not something that is a given or automatically bestowed upon us like rain from the sky or the warmth of the sun on our skin. Instead, happiness is something that we have to choose for ourselves because it takes hard work and effort to achieve and maintain over the long term.

It is important to cultivate a good habit of being genuinely happy for others and happiness will never be too far from you. Happiness is contagious and the more we share it, the more likely we are to see it in our own lives.

If we stay connected to the feeling of gratitude and happiness through this process, then we will be able to see it not only in others but ourselves as well.

Gratitude is a powerful state of mind that can have a profound impact on our lives. When we are grateful for what we have, we are more likely to attract more good into our lives. Gratitude is also a great way to boost our mood and increase our overall happiness.

When you're **free from the noise** of your doubts, discontent, and self-induced drama, you'll know that you are in an evolved state.

You'll always know when you're experiencing **a higher state of consciousness.** No one needs to tell you.

Revenge is never satisfying. It never fills the emptiness inside. It may give us a momentary sense of satisfaction, but it never lasts. In the end, we are left with nothing but a hollow feeling inside.

Joy

*Try rejecting worry
and happiness will pursue you.*

Giving back as often as you can will not only change your life, but also intoxicate you with joy.

We get so wrapped up in our own lives that we often forget about the impact we can have on others.

But when we take the time to give back, it can be one of the most rewarding experiences we can have. It feels good to know that we are making a difference in the lives of others.

Giving back doesn't have to be a big gesture. Every little bit helps, and it all adds up.

When we make giving back a part of our regular routine, we not only improve our own lives, but we also make the world a better place.

We become more compassionate and caring people, and we can't help but feel JOY when we see the positive difference we are making in the lives of others.

COURAGE

FEAR NOT WHAT FEAR WHISPERS TO YOU
FEAR YOUR SUBMISSION TO IT!

Courage

Imagine the success if our determination was as persistent as our problems.

If you're anything like me, you're always looking for ways to improve your life and make things better. And one of the best ways to do that is to learn from your mistakes and keep moving forward.

That's why I'm always so inspired by people who have overcome huge obstacles in their lives. They didn't give up, even when things were tough. And that's what I want to focus on today. Many of us give up too easily. We get discouraged when things don't go our way and we don't see results immediately. But if we could just be a little more determined, we could achieve so much more.

So, today, I challenge you to think about something you really want to achieve. And then, make a plan to go after it with everything you've got. Don't give up, no matter what.

I promise you, it will be worth it in the end.

The eartHeart Knows Who You Are

It seems like every day, we're bombarded with problems. Whether it's something at work, at home, or in our personal lives, it can feel like we're constantly fighting an uphill battle. But what if our determination was as strong as our problems? Imagine the success we could achieve!

No matter how dull or dark the situation is, let's live the best we can with what we have, even if we think it's nothing, for **life is the greatest something**. We all have our ups and downs, our light moments and our dark moments. Sure, there will be times when we feel like we have nothing to live for.

But even in those moments, let's remember that we always have life itself. And as long as we have life, **we have the potential for happiness and joy**.

So no matter how dark or dull the situation is, let's try to **make the best of it**. Let's live our lives to the fullest, even if we think we have nothing. Because in reality, we have the greatest something – life itself.

Courage

If you must bear false witness, then fear has found you.

The eartHeart Knows Who You Are

You know what they say, "Whatever you can do, then do it well." And I completely agree! If you want to be successful in anything you do, you have to **give it your all and then some**.

Sure, there will be times when you feel like you are unable to do it or just not good enough. Those are the times when you have to **be extra persistent and push through those negative thoughts**. It's worth it.

And once you've achieved success, don't forget to enjoy the ride. As they say, **"success is a jealous lover."** So savor every moment and let yourself be consumed by your love affair with success.

It all starts with taking that first step and giving it your all. Whatever you're pursuing in life, **go after it with everything you've got**. And I promise you, success will eventually be yours.

Courage

Life would be meaningless without mistakes.
Be not afraid to make them.

Without mistakes, society would have not benefited from so many discoveries. This may sound like a controversial statement, but hear me out. If it weren't for people making mistakes, we would never have made any progress. We would never have learned from our mistakes, and we would never have been able to improve upon them.

Take for example, the Wright brothers. If they hadn't kept trying after their initial failed attempts at flight, we may never have gotten off the ground. Literally.

Or think about the early days of the automobile. If the first few cars hadn't been so faulty and prone to breaking down, we might never have figured out how to make them better.
In each of these cases, and in countless others, it was

only through making mistakes that we were able to learn and grow. We discovered new things and we found ways to make them better. So next time you make a mistake, don't be too hard on yourself. Remember, it just might be the key to making a great discovery.

Courage

There is an unseen power that helps us when we are free from the fear of making mistakes.

The eartHeart Knows Who You Are

Perfection is an ideal that we can never fully achieve. It's important to remember that it doesn't exist. Though chasing after it can be tempting, it's ultimately a fruitless endeavour.

However, we should not be afraid to make mistakes. We all know that feeling: the sinking sensation in the pit of your stomach when you realize you've made a mistake.

Whether it's a small error or a major faux pas, **it's natural to feel upset and even embarrassed**. It's important to remember that making mistakes is an essential part of being human.

While mistakes can be frustrating, they also offer us valuable opportunities for experience, knowledge, and wisdom.

So next time you find yourself feeling down about a mistake, try to see it as a chance to learn and grow.

Courage

Don't allow anyone to throw you off, or flip your switch off. Know that they are really too small in the grand scheme of things.

The eartHeart Knows Who You Are

The enemy is relentless when the true self is awakened, so do not fear obstacles or distractions, as they are as natural as friction is to movement. We can't grow without them, and they're designed to help us win. **The proof is in you**.

Be patient and learn. Recall your journey and what you have overcome.

Believe that this too shall pass.

Everything in life is a cycle. There are ups and downs, but eventually, things will turn around. So don't give up. **Keep going**.

I know it's hard when you feel like you have nothing left. But this is just **the start of something beautiful**.

No matter how difficult it gets, remember that you have so much potential and so much ahead of you. Stay strong and keep going. Everything will work out in the end.

Courage

We cannot achieve more than we think is possible.
Perhaps this is why so many have only achieved way
below their potential.

The first step to achieving anything is believing that it's possible. If you don't believe you can do something, you'll never even try. And if you never try, you'll never succeed. So many people never achieve their potential because they don't believe they can. They sell themselves short and settle for mediocrity.

But you're not like that. You know you're capable of great things. You just need to believe it, too.

There are a number of reasons why we may have only achieved a fraction of what we are capable of, but it is clear that our thoughts play an integral role in shaping the life we lead.

Those who have accomplished more than they ever thought possible have often attributed their success to believing in themselves and refusing to settle for less.

Whether it's staying late at work or meeting with a mentor, there is no limit to what we can accomplish if we believe in our own potential and refuse to let others define what is possible for us.

It is not enough to believe this is true. You have to know it is true.

Courage

*Often it is not that the
anchor is holding on to you. It is you who is
holding on to the anchor.*

Be Kind To Yourself – Be Present – Be Mindful

When you're in the moment, you're not thinking about the past or the future. You're not worried about what other people think of you. You're not worried about what you should be doing. You're just present. It sounds so simple, but it's actually very difficult to do. We are constantly bombarded with distractions that pull us out of the moment. Our phones are ringing, emails are pinging, and we're constantly thinking about what we need to do next.

True presence is about being fully in the moment, without any distractions. It's about being completely focused on what you're doing, and being present in your interactions with others. When you're present, you're more likely to notice the little things that make life beautiful. You're more likely to appreciate the moment, and the people you're sharing it with.

If you're finding it difficult to be present, there are a few things you can do to help yourself.

First, turn off all distractions. Put down your phone, and step away from your computer. If you can, find a quiet place to sit, and just focus on your breath.

Second, focus on your senses. What do you see, hear, and feel in the moment? Really take in your surroundings, and savour the experience.

Third, practice mindfulness. Mindfulness is the act of being fully aware of your thoughts and feelings, without judgment. When you're mindful, you're able to observe your thoughts and feelings, without getting caught up in them. Practicing mindfulness can help you to be more present in the moment. There are many different ways to practice mindfulness, so find one that works for you.

Fourth, be kind to yourself. If you find yourself getting caught up in your thoughts, or you're having trouble being present, don't be hard on yourself. Just gently bring your attention back to the present moment.

True presence is a state of mind that takes practice. But the more you focus on being present, the easier it will become. And the more present you are, the more you'll be able to enjoy the beauty of life.

Start by making a conscious effort to be present in your life, and then keep at it.

With time and practice, you'll be able to develop a deeper sense of presence.

Leap as if you were pushed!
Sometimes it is the only way to make the next step.

The eartHeart Knows Who You Are

Guard your confidence. No amount of knowledge, intelligence, or wisdom can be effective without it.

Courage

It is our interpretation of 'NO' that really causes anxiety, pain, and stress.

Arrogance may be at the root of why we find it difficult to forgive others when they have wronged us.

We may feel that we are better than them and that they don't deserve our forgiveness.

Or, we may simply not want to let go of the anger and pain that we feel. Whatever the reason, holding onto unforgiveness can only hurt us in the end.

Letting go of the grudge may be the best way to achieve peace and understanding.

Forgive me for my trespasses, as I forgive those who trespass against me.

Fill me with grace that I may love unconditionally.

Strengthen me, comfort me, and forgive me my doubts as my heart is heavy and gets weary even when I know what must be.

Introspection ...
Take a deep breath and try to be calm. If there's something to regret and resent in the mirror, there's also something in there to acknowledge and admire.

Courage

*Be patient. What is meant for you
may be delayed but not denied.*

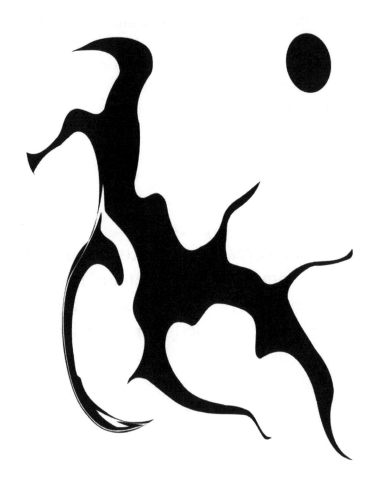

Storms come to pass and do not last.

It's been a tough few months. You've been through a lot of storms and you're feeling pretty down. Don't despair! The storms will eventually end and you will be able to ride them out. **No storm can outlast you.**

You're a strong person and you've been through a lot. You can handle anything that comes your way. So, don't give up when the going gets tough.

Just keep moving forward, one step at a time. The sun will shine again and you will be able to enjoy the peace and beauty of the world around you.

The cost of freedom is the courage to take the next step despite the pain.

Courage

Freedom is never believing what you think they are thinking about you.

Jeanne Vodelle sat with her palms on her knees in a straight-back chair opposite me.

"Tell me, Jeanne, how are you coping, and when last have you taken the time to be still?"

She cleared her throat and swallowed. "It's been a long time since I've taken a break. A really long time. I can't even remember the last time I had a weekend off, let alone a week. And it's not like I don't love my job – I do. I'm passionate about what I do. But lately, I've been feeling like I'm running on empty.

"I'm always exhausted, both physically and emotionally. I'm constantly juggling a million different things and I never seem to have enough time for anything. I know I need to take a step back and recharge, but I feel like I can't.

"Like I said, I love my job. But lately, it's been feeling more like a job and less like a passion. I'm starting to dread going to work. I'm starting to resent the time I'm away from my family and friends.

The eart**H**eart Knows Who You Are

"I know I need to take some time for myself, but I don't know how. I don't know how to take a break when there's so much to do.

"But I'm starting to realize that if I don't take a break soon, I'm going to burn out. And I don't want to do that. I don't want to lose my passion for what I do. I don't want to lose my love for my job."

"So, what will you do?"

Her gaze met mine. "Great question, Selwyn."

She adjusted her scarf and moistened her lips. "I'm going to take a break," she began. "A real break. I'm going to take some time for myself. I'm going to recharge. I'm going to breathe. I'm going to give myself permission to be human."

"And even when it's hard, even when I'm doubted, I'm going to remind myself that I'm worth it. That I deserve this."

"Because I do."

Courage

Know that when your energy threatens someone's significance, they can become a secret enemy.

"I chose risk because doubt was overcrowded."

Courage

Forgive them now that you know
it will set you free.

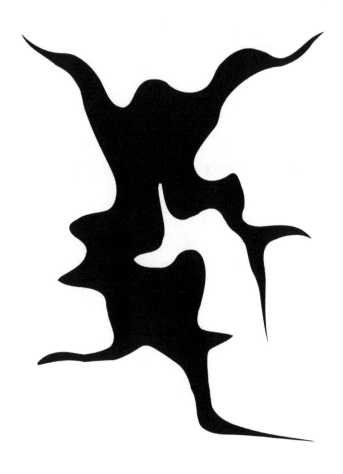

The eartHeart Knows Who You Are

*I have faith, I believe that the Lord is my shepherd.
Then why do I hesitate, doubt, and have wants?*

You are not alone in feeling this way. There's nothing wrong with needing a little reminder now and then that we're on the right track. Sometimes our humanity can get the best of us and we can feel lost and alone. But that's okay!

We can always turn to something bigger than ourselves for guidance and reassurance. Whether that's a higher power, nature, or simply a trusted friend or family member, seeking comfort from outside sources is a perfectly normal and healthy part of life.

I'm sure we've all been there. You're in the middle of a tough situation and you start to doubt yourself. You question your abilities and wonder if you can really make it through. But what if I told you that it's okay to ask for help? That it's okay to seek forgiveness, guidance, and comfort from a higher power?

Everythig works out in the end.

Courage

The good thing about being the writer and editor of your life is that you control the punctuations.

Courage is what will push us to keep going when things get tough. It is what will motivate us to keep going even when we feel like we can't. Courage is the power that will help us get through to the end.

You have decided to begin your journey toward self-discovery. On this journey, you may discover things about yourself that you never knew before.

You may come to understand your deepest desires and fears. You may even find your purpose in life. But most importantly, you'll come to know yourself in a way you have never before.

The eartHeart Knows Who You Are

It is unwise to reveal your ideas while they are still in the womb.

Courage

*How can I be ordinary when I
seek extraordinary things?*

**Humanity may not excuse messing up,
but it explains it.**

Only someone who is ignorant of their own greatness and true power has the fortitude to be envious of others.

Some people are determined to extinguish flames, abort ideas, and kill dreams and joy.
But you were created to be better.
You can vibrate at a higher frequency.
You have the choice and power to do so.

Courage

*How can negativity ever find me
in this maze of accomplishments?*

Your burdens have grown heavier with time. You have been carrying them for a while, and now they are too much to bear. **It's time to let go and be who you were created to be.**

The eartHeart Knows Who You Are

Don't worry about those who resent your brilliance. Though many may despise you, none can extinguish your inner flame.

Your light is a beacon of hope in the darkness, a reminder that no matter how bleak things may seem, there is always a way to find the beauty in life.

Those who resent your light may try to extinguish it. They will never succeed. **Your light is too strong and too powerful**. It comes from a place of love, courage, and hope. It can never be extinguished.

So, don't worry about those who resent your brilliance. They can never extinguish your light.

Be never afraid to shine.

Courage

As the director of your own life
you can always change the script.

Even though familiarity may blind others to your potential, it is your doubts and inhibitions that **blind you to your greatness**.

Who are you to give in to doubts and fears, and **delay your purpose**? Who are you to deny us your unique gifts?

The eartHeart Knows Who You Are

Making mistakes is a natural part of life. We all do it, and it's nothing to be ashamed of. In fact, making mistakes is how we learn and grow. There's a difference between making a mistake and being afraid to make one. The latter can hold us back from living our best lives.

When we're afraid of making mistakes, we're usually afraid of two things: judgement and failure. We worry that others will judge us harshly if we make a mistake, and that we'll fail if we don't do everything perfectly. Neither of these things are true.

Yes, people may judge us if we make a mistake. They'll also judge us if we're afraid to take risks and try new things. And, more importantly, they'll judge us more harshly if we judge ourselves.

So, if you're afraid of making mistakes, remember this: you're not alone, and you're not a failure. We all make mistakes, and that's okay. What's not okay is letting our fear of making mistakes hold us back from living our lives to the fullest.

Courage

Where arrogance prevails, opinions will always be louder than truth.

Success comes from being in the now. It comes from being present in each moment. So often, we get stuck on what was, could have been, might have been, should have been, and ignore the power of what is.

Life is a collection of moments. So, do not waste this moment with terrifying thoughts of the past or the future.

You have crossed precipices, escaped chasms, and survived storms, so you can handle what comes next. The obstacles ahead cannot defeat you. They are only reminders of your greatness.

The eartHeart Knows Who You Are

**Every moment is perfect,
but for my thoughts.**

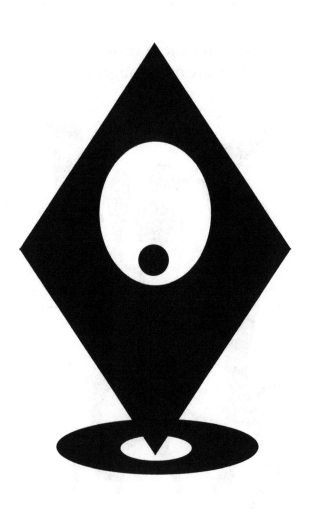

I Am En

LET OTHERS BE AS THEY ARE
SO THAT YOU MIGHT BE AS YOU ARE.

I Am En

You're a gifted mystery, and the sum of all you have ever chosen to be. Know that YOU are enough.

The eartHeart Knows Who You Are

Some people are determined to be flame dousers, idea destroyers, and dreams and joy killers.

You might know some who have given up on themselves and others, and refuse to believe that their hearts, like glowing embers, can ignite and sing again.

Be not like this.
You were created to be better.
You can vibrate higher.
You have a choice and you have will.

Be still and know...
You can make a difference if you try.
Stop pretending that you can't.
You're not a victim.

Be a blessing to yourself and others.
Encourage others.
Love, give, and forgive.
Be kind.

I Am En.

I Am En

Do not be lazy. Do your shadow work. Do whatever it takes to identify your triggers and do some research into your past to find out what childhood trauma might have started it.

When it comes to personal growth and development, there is no such thing as being "lazy." In order to truly improve ourselves, we must be willing to put in the hard work required to identify our triggers and do the necessary research to discover any childhood trauma that might have started them.

It can be easy to fall into the trap of thinking that we can just "wing it" when it comes to personal growth, but the truth is that this approach rarely leads to lasting change. If we want to make lasting improvements in our lives, it is essential that we take the time to do the shadow work required to uncover our triggers and understand the root causes of our issues.

This can be a difficult and painful process, but it is

one that is essential if we want to heal our wounds and become our best selves. So, if you're feeling stuck in a rut and are ready to make some real changes in your life, don't be lazy - do the work required to discover your triggers and start healing your wounds. It might not be easy, but it will be worth it in the end.

Someone asked me, "Why did you have to make such a difficult choice?" I replied, "Why do you assume I saw both choices and the other was easier?"

If you want to achieve greatness, you need to put pressure on yourself and be willing to face challenges.

I Am En

You've been through a lot, but have you made it through?
Have you learnt the lesson? Did you take the time to ask?

The eartHeart Knows Who You Are

It is I who found you and awaits you to find me.

I found you when you were lost and alone.
I found you in the darkness and brought you into the light.

I found you in your time of need and offered you my help. I am always here for you, waiting for you to find me.

I am the one who loves you unconditionally.
I will never forsake you.
I am your friend and your companion.
I will never leave you.

I am the one who will always be there for you.
I am your strength and your hope.
I will never let you down.
I am the one who found you.
I will always be waiting for you to find me.

I Am En

I Am En

Bid me not against my nature
for I am the now and the after.

The eartHeart Knows Who You Are

If you are imagining or seeing something that is not in existence, that means you're supposed to bring it into existence. It waits for you to overcome your fear and believe in what you need to do.

Be still and know...
You can make a difference if you try.
Stop pretending that you can't.
You're not a victim.
Be a blessing to yourself and others,
Encourage others.
Love, give, and forgive.
Be kind.

It is I who found you
and awaits you to find me.
I Am En.

ABOUT THE AUTHOR

Selwyn Collins is an award-winning author and entrepreneur who is committed to motivating, inspiring, encouraging, and supporting others. His seminars and forums are designed to enhance and improve communities. He is the founder of Brand YOUth Global Inc., which is dedicated to elevating mindsets and empowering individuals for sustainable socio-economic upliftment in Guyana.

Additionally, he has incorporated the Women of Brand YOUth (W.O.B.Y.) into his work, which speaks to his passion for empowering women and to the growth of equality in Guyana. In 2018, he hosted International Women's Day in Guyana and continues his commitment to supporting women through his International Women's Forum and Brand YOUth Global. He was also the architect of Brand YOUth's Entrepreneurial Tax Forum for small and medium-sized businesses in Guyana. His creative media skills led to his online forum, Conversations With Selwyn (CWS), which is an archival library of life stories.

Collins is constantly coming up with creative ways to support others and improve the world around him. He is a friendly and inspiring presence that always has the best intentions at heart.

Lightning Source UK Ltd.
Milton Keynes UK
UKHW022007051222
413454UK00021B/354